Usborne Beginners
Dogs

Emma Helbrough
Designed by Josephine Thompson

Illustrated by Patrizia Donaera and Uwe Mayer

Dog consultant: Emma Milne

Reading consultant: Alison Kelly
Roehampton University of Surrey

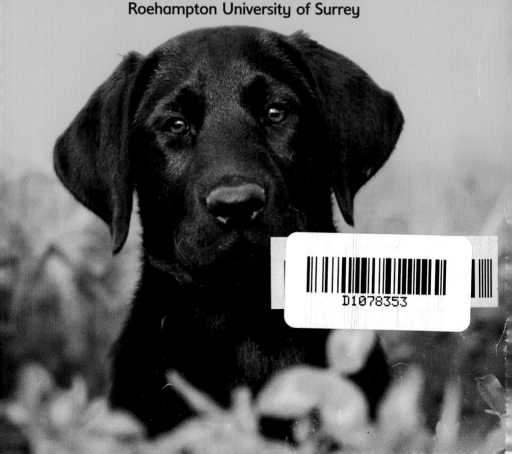

Contents

Different dogs

There are lots of different kinds of dogs.
Some are very big, but others are tiny.
They can have long fur or short fur.

This spotted dog is
called a Dalmatian.

Puppies

Mother dogs usually give birth to between six and ten puppies. They sleep close together to keep warm.

A group of puppies is called a litter.

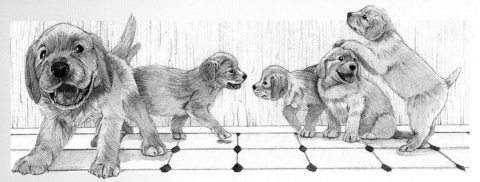

Puppies begin to walk at two weeks old.
They like to explore as they get older.

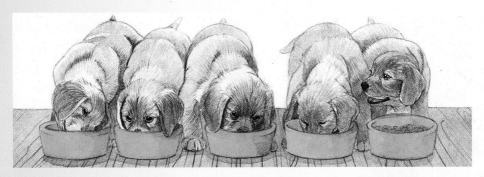

Puppies grow their first teeth at three
weeks old and begin to eat solid food.

They start to grow their adult teeth at four
months old and like to chew things.

Playtime

Puppies start to play together when they are about three weeks old.

Puppies like to play-fight. They jump on top of each other to show who is strongest.

Dogs often chase each other around parks. They take turns being chased.

Some dogs live in the wild. Wolves are
wild dogs. Their pups play like pet puppies.

Pet puppies chase after
things for fun.

Wild pups chase too but
they are learning to hunt.

In the pack

Dogs like to be with people or other dogs.

Wolves live in groups called packs.

There can be up to fifteen wolves in a pack. One of the wolves is the pack leader. The other wolves follow their leader's orders.

Pet dogs think their owner is their pack leader.

A dog greets its pack leader by licking its face.

Then it lies on its back to show it knows who is boss.

Puppies often play as if they are in a pack.

One of the puppies is always more bossy than the rest. It acts as the pack leader.

On guard

A dog's home and the area around it is called its territory.

Dogs think they own their territory, so they guard it.

They bark when strangers come near.

Basenjis are the only kind of dog that can't bark.

Dogs wet around their territory to leave their smell behind.

When a dog sniffs an area it can tell if it belongs to another dog.

Dogs try to take over each other's territory.

A dog sniffs a post where another dog has already been.

Then it wets the post to cover up the other dog's smell.

Dog talk

Dogs make lots of noises but they use their face and body to show how they feel too.

A dog wags its tail quickly when it is happy or excited.

It growls and shows its teeth when it is very angry.

It pricks its ears up when it is interested in something.

It puts its tail between its legs if it thinks it is in trouble.

12

WOOO O O C O C

Some dogs howl if they are left alone. They are calling to their owner.

This dog wants to play. It has put its front legs down and its bottom in the air.

This is called a play-bow.

Digging

Dogs like to dig for fun but they dig for lots of other reasons too.

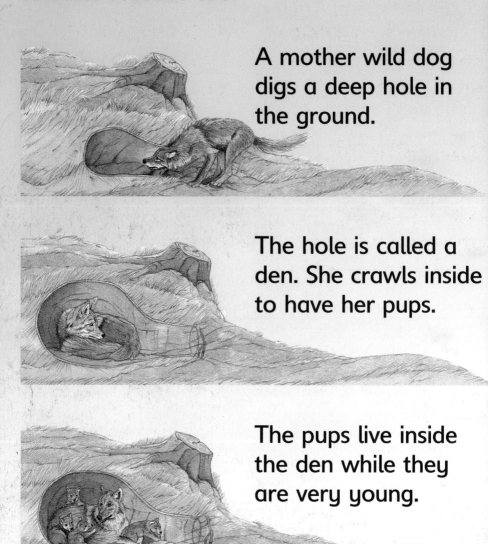

A mother wild dog digs a deep hole in the ground.

The hole is called a den. She crawls inside to have her pups.

The pups live inside the den while they are very young.

On a hot day, some dogs dig a hole in the ground.

Then they lie in the hole because it's cooler there.

Dogs often bury their toys to keep them safe. They dig them up when they want to play.

In the wild

Wild dogs hunt for food in packs. Their young pups stay behind in the den.

These African wild dog pups are waiting for their pack to return from hunting.

African wild dogs live in hot places, so they spend most of the day resting in the shade.

On a hunt, a pack of African wild dogs creeps up on a group of zebras.

The zebras scatter when they see the dogs. The dogs begin to chase one of the zebras.

When the zebra gets tired, the dogs catch it and gather around to eat it.

Sniffing around

Dogs have an amazing sense of smell. They can tell more about something by smelling it than by looking at it.

Dogs sniff each other when they meet.

They can tell how old another dog is and if it's a male or a female just by sniffing it.

After a dog has been given a bath, its fur smells different.

So it rolls in smelly things to cover up the new smell.

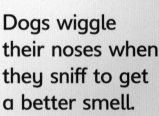

Dogs wiggle their noses when they sniff to get a better smell.

Bloodhounds have the best sense of smell. It is thousands of times better than yours.

Search and rescue

Dogs use their good sense of smell to help people find things and find other people.

At airports trained dogs sniff people's bags.

They find things that people are not allowed to take on planes, such as animals and weapons.

After an earthquake dogs help rescue teams search through the rubble.

Rescue teams use dogs to find people who are lost on mountains.

A dog can smell if someone is trapped under the snow.

The dog barks when it finds someone and the team digs them out.

Clever helpers

Some dogs are trained to help people who can't hear or see very well.

Hearing dogs tell their owner if they hear a sound, such as an alarm clock.

The dog touches its owner with a paw when it hears a sound.

If it hears a smoke alarm, the dog lies down to show danger.

If it hears a doorbell, the dog then leads its owner to the door.

Guide dogs help people who can't see well to travel safely.

The dogs are trained to lead their owner around things.

They learn to wait at the edge of a road until it is safe to cross.

Sheepdogs

Farmers use dogs to round up sheep in fields.

A kind of dog called a border collie is often used as a sheepdog.

This puppy will start training to be a sheepdog when it is six months old.

Sheepdogs can also be trained to round up cows, goats and even ducks!

The farmer uses a whistle and shouts to the sheepdog.

The sheepdog creeps behind the sheep and guides them to a sheep pen.

If a sheep strays from the group, the sheepdog runs over to guide it back again.

Sled dogs

Teams of dogs pull sleds across the snow.
Some people use them to travel around.
Other people race them for fun.

Each dog wears a
harness which clips
onto a long line.

Then the line is
joined to the front
of the sled.

The person who drives
the sled is called a musher.

Sled dogs get hungry after running a race.
They eat six times as much food as pet dogs.

The dogs often wear
socks to protect their
paws from the snow.

The musher shouts
"hike" or "let's go"
to start the dogs.

Dog families

If a mother and a father dog look exactly the same, their puppies look the same too. They are called purebreds.

These old English sheepdog puppies will grow up to look like their parents.

If a mother and a father dog don't look the same...

...their puppies look like a mixture of both of them.

Dogs that are a mixture of different kinds are called mixed breeds.

Mixed breed dogs are often more healthy and live longer than purebred dogs.

Glossary of dog words

Here are some of the words in this book you might not know. This page tells you what they mean.

 pups - another word for puppies. Wild dog puppies are often called pups.

 pack - a group of dogs. Wild dogs live in packs.

 pack leader - the dog that is in charge of all the other dogs in a pack.

 territory - the place where a dog lives. Dogs guard their territory.

 den - the place where wild pups are born and live when they are very small.

 harness - a special strap that a dog sometimes wears.

 sheepdog - a dog that is trained to round up sheep.

Websites to visit

If you have a computer, you can find out more about dogs on the Internet. On the Usborne Quicklinks Website there are links to four fun websites.

Website 1 - Learn how to draw a puppy.

Website 2 - Make dog masks, cards and puppets.

Website 3 - Print pictures of different kinds of dogs to fill in.

Website 4 - Find out more about dogs.

To visit these websites, go to **www.usborne-quicklinks.com** and type the keywords "beginners dogs". Then, click on the link for the website you want to visit. Before you use the Internet, look at the safety guidelines inside the back cover of this book and ask an adult to read them with you.

Index

Acknowledgements

Managing editor: Fiona Watt,
Managing designer: Mary Cartwright
Photographic manipulation: John Russell

Photo credits

The publishers are grateful to the following for permission to reproduce material.
© **Africa Imagery:** 16 (Roger de la Harpe); © **Ardea:** 11, 24 (John Daniels);
© **Frank Lane Picture Agency:** 8 (Tim Fitzharris/Minden Pictures), 23 (Klein/Hubert/FotoNatu
© **Getty:** cover, 29 (Patricia Doyle), 1 (Gary Randall), 2-3 (Geoff du Feu), 19 (Dag Sundberg)
© **ImageState:** 28; © **Leeson Photos:** 7 (Tom & Pat Leeson); © **NHPA:** 4 (E.A. Janes)
9 (Henry Ausloos); © **Powerstock:** 21 (Bob Winsett/Index Stock Imagery);
© **Richard Schiller:** 26-27; © **Warren Photographic:** 6, 10, 18, 31 (Jane Burton),
13 (Kim Taylor); © **Workbookstock:** 15 (Lori Adamski-Peek).